9/16/16
$35.64

jnn

1/17

TOOLS
OF THE TRADE:
USING SCIENTIFIC EQUIPMENT

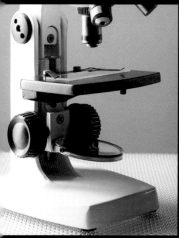

Kirsten Larson

Rourke
Educational Media

rourkeeducationalmedia.com

Scan for Related Titles and Teacher Resources

Before Reading:

Building Academic Vocabulary and Background Knowledge

Before reading a book, it is important to tap into what your child or students already know about the topic. This will help them develop their vocabulary, increase their reading comprehension, and make connections across the curriculum.

1. *Look at the cover of the book. What will this book be about?*
2. *What do you already know about the topic?*
3. *Let's study the Table of Contents. What will you learn about in the book's chapters?*
4. *What would you like to learn about this topic? Do you think you might learn about it from this book? Why or why not?*
5. *Use a reading journal to write about your knowledge of this topic. Record what you already know about the topic and what you hope to learn about the topic.*
6. *Read the book.*
7. *In your reading journal, record what you learned about the topic and your response to the book.*
8. *After reading the book complete the activities below.*

Content Area Vocabulary
Read the list. What do these words mean?

atoms
data
electron
genes
hypothesis
infrasonic
lens
mass
molecule
observation
slide
specimen
theory
variables
volume

After Reading:

Comprehension and Extension Activity

After reading the book, work on the following questions with your child or students in order to check their level of reading comprehension and content mastery.

1. *Describe some discoveries that were only possible once the right tools existed.* (Summarize)
2. *How would the work of scientists be different without tools?* (Infer)
3. *How can everyday household items be used as tools for discovery?* (Asking questions)
4. *What tools do you use at home and school?* (Text to self connection)
5. *In what ways have computers changed the ways scientists approach their research?* (Asking questions)

Extension Activity

Art and science may seem unrelated, but in reality, there is science in art and art in science. Now it's time for you to think artistically. Write a poem about the scientific process, using as many vocabulary words from the book that you can. You can write it from your own point of view, or create a character that is discovering something new. Get creative!

Table of Contents

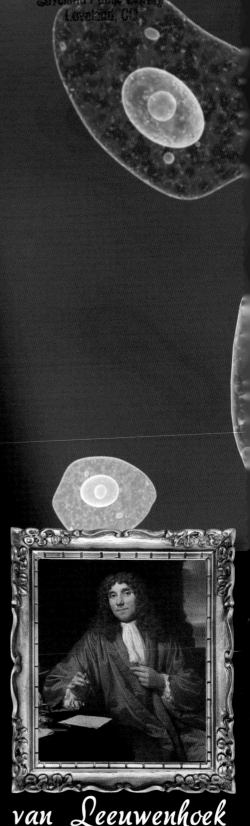

Tools of Discovery

In 1676, Antonie van Leeuwenhoek peered at a drop of water through a magnifying **lens** he made himself. Using this scientific tool, the self-taught scientist made an amazing discovery: tiny creatures he called animalcules. They were protozoa, single-celled creatures. No one had seen them before.

Originally a cloth merchant, van Leeuwenhoek probably used magnifying glasses to examine cloth as part of his business. The tool helped merchants look at threads up close and determine the cloth's quality. Eventually, van Leeuwenhoek became obsessed with making ever more powerful magnification devices. His lenses were capable of magnifying objects over 200 times, making them far more powerful than microscopes used at the time.

van Leeuwenhoek
1632 – 1723

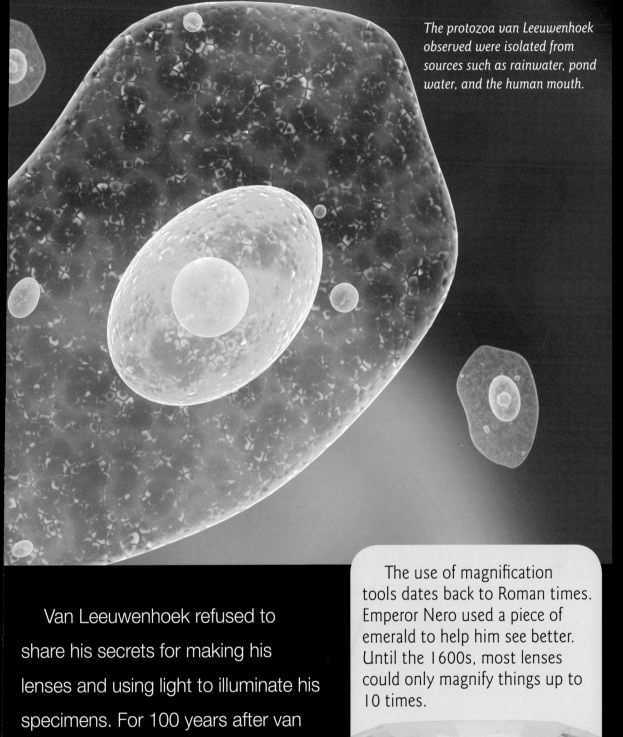

The protozoa van Leeuwenhoek observed were isolated from sources such as rainwater, pond water, and the human mouth.

Van Leeuwenhoek refused to share his secrets for making his lenses and using light to illuminate his specimens. For 100 years after van Leeuwenhoek died in 1723, no one saw his animalcules again.

The use of magnification tools dates back to Roman times. Emperor Nero used a piece of emerald to help him see better. Until the 1600s, most lenses could only magnify things up to 10 times.

Uranus

Herschel began his telescope-making career in 1773 by experimenting with relatively small refractors, but certainly not in length – one of them was 30 feet (9.14 meters) long!

Tools help scientists not only discover new creatures, but also distant worlds. Like van Leeuwenhoek, German musician William Herschel built his own scientific tools with the help of his sister, Caroline. Their home-built telescopes were far more powerful than those they could buy.

In 1781, Herschel made his first discovery–the planet Uranus. Most people thought the planet was a star, but seeing more clearly with his telescope, Herschel saw it was a planet.

William Herschel
1738 – 1822

Herschel's research did not stop there. Through the years, he cataloged nebulae, nurseries where stars are born, and studied the sun, moon, and planets within our solar system. He determined that Saturn's rings are really made of particles. Without powerful telescopes, these distant worlds would have remained a mystery.

In the hands of William Herschel, the telescope became a powerful scientific tool. The telescope displayed here was Herschel's favorite: his 20-foot (6.1 meter) reflector.

Hans Lippershey
1570 – 1619

Quite a Visionary

Hans Lippershey invented the first telescope around 1608. Legend has it that two children playing with lenses in Lippershey's eyeglass shop inspired his invention. Looking through two lenses at once they noticed a weathervane on a church looked much closer. Lippershey attached a lens on either end of a tube, inventing the new science tool.

All scientific tools enhance scientists' natural abilities. Even the hardest-working scientists are limited by how well they can see or hear. Tools such as microscopes, telescopes, and audio equipment improve their abilities. Scientists also can be limited by how well they can detect differences. A scientist might ask, which liquid is hotter? A

Graduated cylinders are a key piece of equipment in a scientific laboratory. They are critical for measuring liquid volumes when conducting experiments.

thermometer helps scientists know for sure. Still other tools improve a scientist's ability to conduct an experiment. In a lab, graduated cylinders and meter sticks allow them to make exact measurements as they work. This leads to better results. No matter the type, tools of the trade help scientists do their jobs.

The Scientific Method

Scientists use a process called the scientific method to conduct experiments and make discoveries. They use different science tools each step of the way. The five steps of the scientific method are:

1. Observing and asking questions about the world.

2. Researching to learn all you can about your question.

3. Creating a **hypothesis**, a testable answer to the question.

4. Designing and conducting experiments to test the hypothesis.

5. Analyzing results, making conclusions, and sharing the results with others.

Tools for Observation

Science experiments start with careful **observation**, the first step of the scientific method. Observing means studying something carefully using all of your senses: sight, smell, touch, taste, and hearing. Many science tools help scientists improve their observations.

An optical microscope creates a magnified image of an object with an objective lens and magnifies the image even more with an eyepiece that allows the user to observe it with the naked eye.

Seeing better

For thousands of years, people used water, gems, and glass to make objects appear bigger than they are. This allowed scientists to study details they could not see with their naked eye. Today people use microscopes to see smaller and smaller objects, sometimes even individual **atoms**, which are the smallest building blocks of matter.

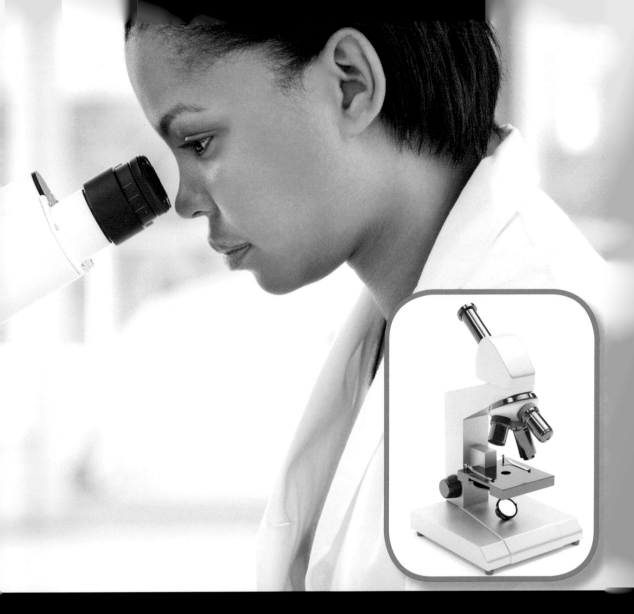

There are several types of microscopes. Optical microscopes, also known as light microscopes, are the most common type. They are found in many school laboratories. Optical microscopes focus light to make objects look larger. The simplest ones have just one lens, which is a piece of plastic or glass for magnifying, much like an eyeglass lens.

Powerful Paper

A Stanford scientist created a paper microscope for less than a dollar. Called the Foldscope, the microscope is bringing science tools to countries where people can't afford expensive equipment.

Most optical microscopes today are compound microscopes, which use two or more lenses. With these, light shines through a **specimen** on a clear **slide**. A lens above the slide magnifies the specimen. A second lens in the eyepiece magnifies the first image. Compound microscopes in school labs can magnify images up to 400 times, while research microscopes may magnify objects 1,000 times. These powerful tools reveal individual red blood cells in a smear of blood.

How A Microscope Works

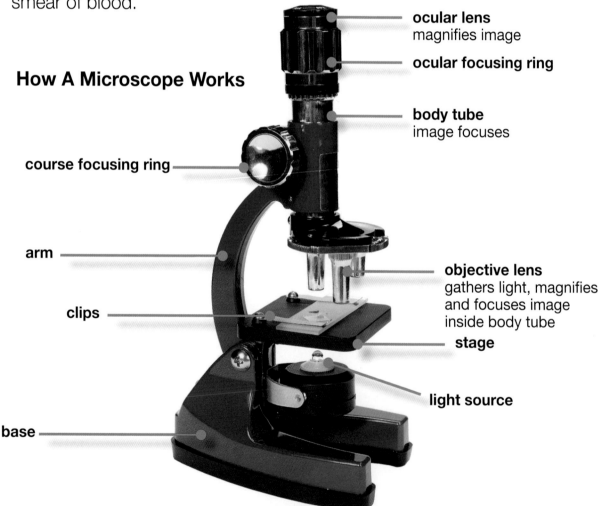

ocular lens
magnifies image

ocular focusing ring

body tube
image focuses

course focusing ring

arm

clips

objective lens
gathers light, magnifies
and focuses image
inside body tube

stage

light source

base

Microscopes used in homes, schools, and professional laboratories are actually compound microscopes and use at least two lenses to produce a magnified image. The objective lens is above the object and another lens, called an ocular lens, is the eyepiece used to view the specimen.

Using a Microscope

When using a microscope, first secure the glass slide using the clips. Choose your magnification setting by rotating the lens above the specimen. Using the focusing knob, move the lens as close to the slide as possible without touching it. Then move the focusing knob slowly until the object on the slide comes into view.

For simple and compound microscopes, samples must be sliced thinly so the light can shine through. For thicker specimens, scientists may turn to microscopes that use laser beams and project 3D images on a screen.

Electron microscopes use electrons, tiny parts of atoms, instead of light to make the image. They allow scientists to see 1,000 times better than an optical microscope. Electron microscopes can show individual snowflakes or grains of pollen.

Electron microscopes are large, expensive pieces of equipment, generally standing alone in a small, specially designed room. They require trained personnel to operate them.

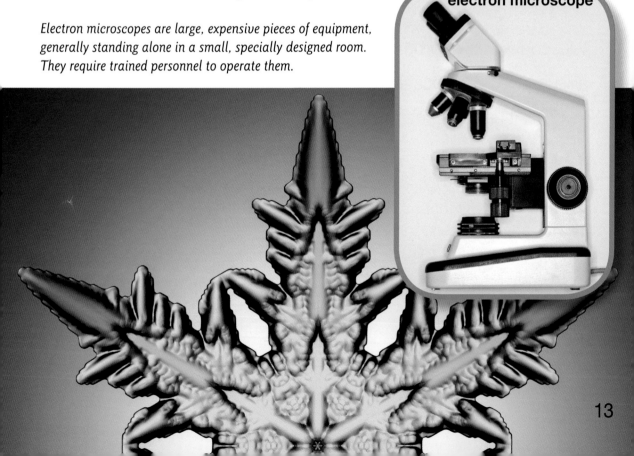

electron microscope

13

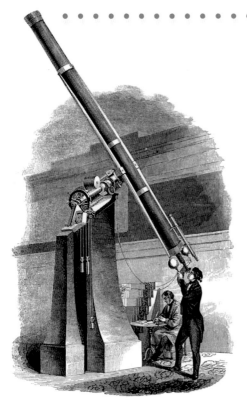

The Yerkes Observatory telescope was the world's largest telescope from 1897 to 1909, and it is still the world's largest refractor.

While biologists use microscopes to make nearby specimens appear larger, astronomers use telescopes to collect light and make far away objects look closer. The more light a telescope captures, the more powerful it is.

The earliest telescopes were refracting telescopes. A glass lens inside the telescope bent light and focused the image. The eyepiece magnified the image. Because the glass lenses can only be supported from the side, like the lenses on a pair of eyeglasses, these telescopes can only be made so big. The biggest refracting telescope still used today is located at the Yerkes Observatory in Wisconsin. Built in 1897, it has a 40 inch (one meter) glass lens, which is about the size of a semi-truck's tire.

More modern telescopes are reflecting telescopes. They replace glass lenses with mirrors. The mirrors can be supported from behind, not just from the sides. This means the mirrors can be made even bigger than glass lenses to collect more light.

Did You Know?

The word telescope comes from the Greek word *tele*, meaning "far," and *skopein*, meaning "to view."

The Las Campanas Observatory in Chile uses two mirrors that make it as powerful as a telescope with a 300-foot (91-meter) mirror, almost the size of a football field.

Las Campanas Observatory

View from Above

Other telescopes use the portions of light we can't see to magnify objects. They use radio, infrared, ultraviolet or gamma waves. Some of these telescopes, such as the Chandra X-Ray Observatory, are satellites circling the Earth and peering into space. NASA even operates an infrared telescope that flies aboard a modified 747 airliner.

Reflector telescopes are less expensive to make than refractor telescopes of the same size.

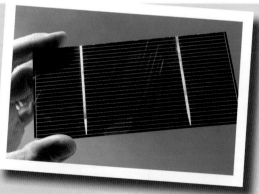

The National Oceanic and Atmospheric Administration (NOAA) designed and built Hercules. Equipped with special features that allow it to perform intricate tasks, it can also descend to depths of 4,000 meters (2.5 miles).

Cameras and video cameras are two other tools that help scientists observe. Often they allow scientists to observe in places they can't travel, like deep in the ocean or on distant planets. Another advantage is the camera's ability to record images and sounds for playback over and over again.

Power Tools

Scientists who use video cameras in the field have faced a constant problem: what to do when the batteries die. Now inventors have created a camera that can run on solar power: no regular batteries required.

Solar-powered items use solar cells to convert the energy of light directly into electricity.

NASA's Curiosity Mars Rover captures high definition images of the Red Planet. Not long after landing, the rover took images of rocks that contained fine grains of sand and rounded pebbles. These pictures provided clues about Mars's ancient past. Even though Mars has no surface water today, scientists knew only moving water could smooth those smaller, rounded rocks. From the shape and size of the pebbles, scientists concluded flowing, hip-high water must have once covered the area.

Curiosity Mars Rover

Scientists also use special audio equipment to observe the world around them. Wildlife biologists use audio recording devices in the field. In Africa, they place waterproof, **infrasonic** sound equipment in trees. The equipment records elephant's vocalizations, many of which are too low pitched for humans to hear. Using these science tools, scientists have learned that elephants use these incredibly low calls to communicate over many miles. The discovery has helped explain how elephants find mates and how extended families communicate when separated.

The Comprehensive Nuclear Test-Ban Treaty Organization (CTBTO) monitors infrasound sound waves at frequencies too low to be detected by the human ear at sites like this in Qaanaaq, Greenland.

Make Your Own Stethoscope

Doctors use stethoscopes to enhance their ability to listen to the body and diagnose disease. Now you can make your own.

What You'll Need

- cardboard tube from a roll of paper towels
- plastic funnel
- duct tape
- scissors

What You'll Do

1. Place the skinny end of the funnel inside the cardboard tube.
2. Cut a piece of duct tape long enough to wrap around the tube a couple of times.
3. Tape the funnel to the tube.
4. To use the stethoscope, place the funnel end against a friend's heart, while placing your ear at the other end of the tube. You can also use your stethoscope to listen for sounds inside trees or anywhere else you can imagine.

Tools for Answering Questions

By the 1950s, scientists learned that a **molecule** called DNA carried a person's **genes**. Genes come from your parents and are the unique recipe for making you. Still, no one knew what DNA looked like or how it passed on genes. Observational tools like microscopes were not yet powerful enough to see a person's DNA. Scientists had to use other tools to learn how it worked.

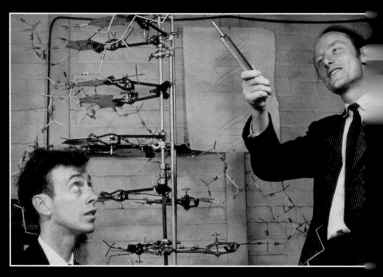

James Watson from Indiana University and Francis Crick from Cambridge University a DNA model using cardboard cutouts fitted together like a puzzle. By 1953, they completed a wire and metal model of DNA, which looked like a twisted ladder called the double helix. Twenty years later, Alexander Rich used x-rays to see DNA for the first time, confirming that Watson and Crick's model was correct.

James Watson and Francis Crick eventual received the Nobel Prize for their discover the structure of DNA.

James Watson

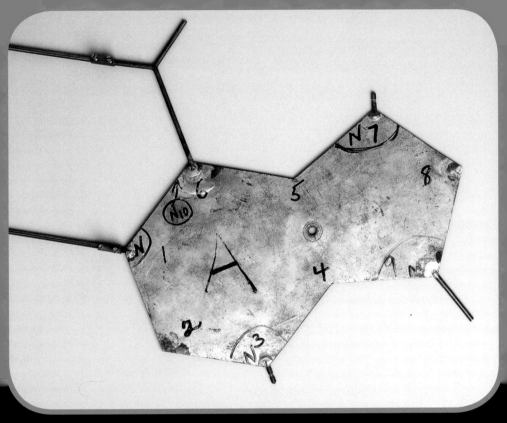

Crick and Watson's model of DNA is represented by
aluminum template representing the base Thymine (

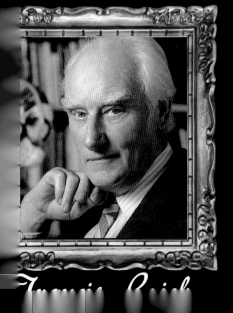

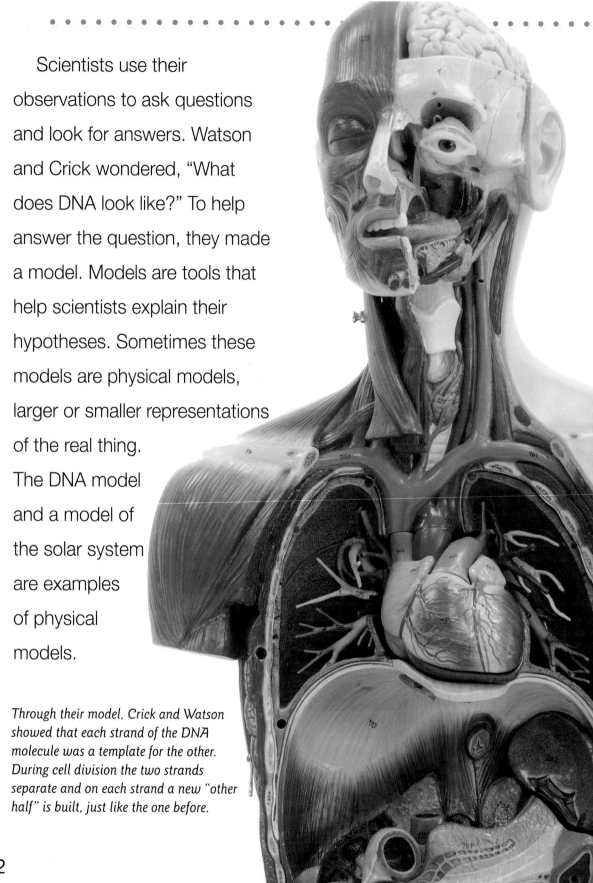

Scientists use their observations to ask questions and look for answers. Watson and Crick wondered, "What does DNA look like?" To help answer the question, they made a model. Models are tools that help scientists explain their hypotheses. Sometimes these models are physical models, larger or smaller representations of the real thing. The DNA model and a model of the solar system are examples of physical models.

Through their model, Crick and Watson showed that each strand of the DNA molecule was a template for the other. During cell division the two strands separate and on each strand a new "other half" is built, just like the one before.

Increasingly, scientists rely upon computer models. Computer models are representations that explain things through a series of mathematical

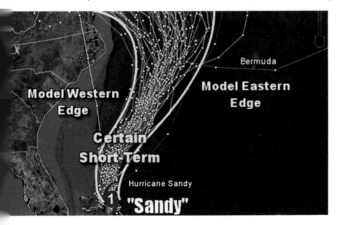

equations. In meteorology, for example, scientists regularly use computer models to predict not just tomorrow's high temperatures, but also where powerful storms like hurricanes might hit.

Sun-sational!

Nicolaus Copernicus was the first to propose a sun-centered model of the solar system, a **theory** he published in 1543.

Earlier models placed the Earth at the center, but those models could not adequately explain the motion of the planets. Later astronomers proved Copernicus correct.

Nicolaus Copernicus
1473 – 1543

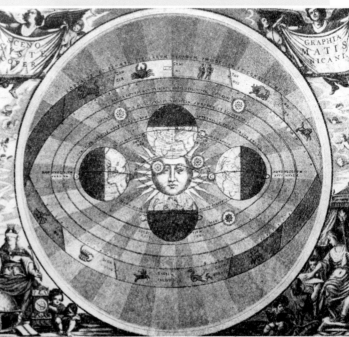

Scientists need lots of **data** for computer models. In meteorology, weather stations and satellites gather information about temperature, wind speed and direction, moisture, and more. This data is fed into a computer. The computer uses mathematical equations to create the prediction. This becomes your local weather forecast.

Computer simulations are special types of models that help scientists understand what might happen under different conditions. They help scientists answer "if … then" questions. For example, a scientist might ask, "If the amount of moisture in the air increases, then how will the path of a hurricane change?" A simulation of the hurricane helps the meteorologist explore how the storm changes based on changes in the weather.

High-Tech Flu Fighters

The flu virus kills up to a half million people around the world each year. Now scientists are hoping a computer simulation will help them beat the virus. The simulation predicts how the flu spreads, as well as how severe outbreaks will be. Using the simulator's predictions, government officials can send vaccines, medicines, doctors, and nurses to the right places at the right time, lessening the virus's impact.

A satellite works by receiving radio signals sent from the Earth and resending the radio signals back down to the Earth. In a simple system, a signal is reflected, or "bounced," off the satellite. Modern communications satellites receive the radio signal and send it back down to Earth stronger than it was received.

Tools for Experimenting

An archerfish swims below the water's surface. When an insect flies nearby, the archerfish spits a stream of water that knocks the potential prey into the water. Gulp! The archerfish devours its meal.

Biologist Morgan Burnette wondered if archerfish changed how hard they hit insects based upon how far away they were from the fish. Do the fish hit far away insects with less force than those nearby? Burnette designed a lab experiment to find out, using three scientific tools: a video camera, a computer, and a compression load cell, which measures the force of the water.

Through his careful measurements, Burnette learned that archerfish spit with the same force no matter how close the prey. Watching the fish on the video camera, Burnette saw that archerfish shoot a stream of water that forms a ball just before impact. By using a variety of tools in a carefully controlled experiment, Burnette has learned a great deal about these amazing animal hunters.

Documenting Discoveries

An important part of performing an experiment is recording how the experiment was set up. Many scientists take photos or videos with cameras to capture this. For students, science fair projects often include pictures of the set up.

This photo was taken to document an experiment on colors' effects on plant growth.

Scientists like Burnette use tools when they experiment. Some tools help them perform the experiment, but don't measure things. Other tools allow scientists to take very accurate measurements during experiments.

Tools scientists use to perform experiments include hot plates, tongs, eyedroppers, and test tubes. Many of these help ensure scientists stay safe in the lab. If flasks or test tubes are hot, using tongs prevents burns. Using eyedroppers when handling dangerous chemicals protects a scientist's hands.

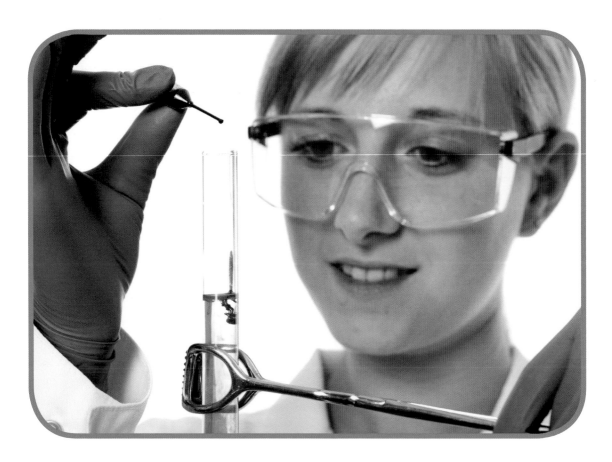

Other tools, like Burnette's load cell, allow scientists to take measurements and collect data. Then they can make careful comparisons. This type of tool includes balances, cylinders, thermometers, meter sticks, and watches.

PREPARE AND PREVENT

One of the best ways to stay safe in the lab is to prepare yourself before you start your experiment. This includes asking yourself about possible dangers and considering what could go wrong. Think about how you would prevent those dangers by using proper safety equipment.

Safety Gear

Many tools keep scientists safe in the lab. Safety goggles protect eyes from dangerous chemicals. Aprons and gloves protect hands and clothing.

Measuring Mass

To measure **mass**, or the amount of matter in an object, scientists use balances. Today's balances can measure masses 10,000 times lighter than a paperclip. Balances date back to ancient Egypt. Ancient Egyptians used balances to weigh items they traded and gold dust, which people used to pay for goods.

Balances typically have a beam and one or more pans. Equal-arm balances resemble a playground seesaw. The object being measured is placed in one pan. The scientist adds weights to the other pan until the beam is level or balanced. Today, many balances are electronic and only use one pan.

Equal-arm balance

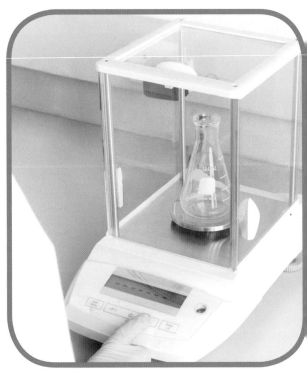

Electronic balance

Measuring Volume

Scientists rely upon several tools to measure **volume**, the amount of space an object takes up. A graduated cylinder is a thin tube with markings. They come in different sizes, including 10 milliliters, 25 milliliters, or 100 milliliters. Graduated cylinders are fairly accurate; however, for even better accuracy, scientists may use pipettes. Pipettes have a bulb at the end. Squeezing the bulb draws liquid into the pipette, like an eyedropper. Scientists release drops of the liquid until the pipette contains just the right amount.

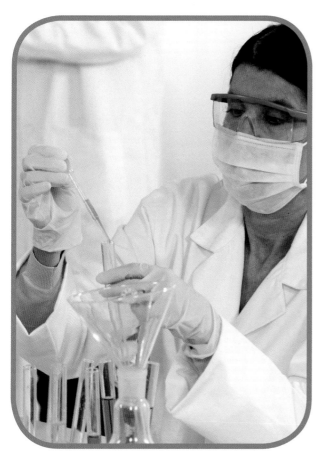

There are several types of pipettes, including manual, autoclavable, reusable and disposable. They can be made of plastic or glass and come in various sizes.

Measure in Metrics

Scientists use the metric system for measurement. The basic measure of mass is a kilogram, while the basic measure of length is a meter. All measurements in the system are based on the number 10. So, for example, there are 10 millimeters in a centimeter, and 10 centimeters in a meter. Before the metric system, people based their measurements on other things. A yard at one time was the measurement from the tip of King Henry I's nose to the end of his thumb.

Measuring Length, Height, or Distance

To measure length, height, or distance, scientists might use meter sticks. A meter stick is a ruler one meter in length and divided into centimeters and millimeters. To take a measurement, the scientist holds the end of the object being measured at zero and notes where the other end falls on the meter stick.

For finer measurements, a scientist may use calipers. The caliper's jaws can be adjusted to match the length or width being measured. They can capture measurements as small as one thousandth of an inch (.002 centimeters).

Calipers are an instrument for measuring thicknesses and internal or external diameters that are inaccessible to a scale, consisting usually of a pair of adjustable pivoted legs.

Measuring Time

When Galileo wanted to compare how quickly balls accelerated down a slope, he didn't have a stopwatch to measure time. Instead, he used one of the earliest types of clocks: the water clock. When he started a ball rolling, Galileo started the water flowing into a container. He stopped the water when the ball stopped. By measuring how much water was in the container, he could compare how long it took the ball to roll different distances. Today scientists use clocks and stopwatches to measure minutes and seconds.

Galileo Galilei
1564 – 1642

Great Timing

Atomic clocks provide the most accurate measurement of time. American Willard Frank Libby invented the atomic clock in 1946. These clocks use the vibration of atoms and molecules to keep time. The most accurate clocks will be off by just one second every 30 billion years.

Chip scale atomic clocks like this one are expected to continuously revolutionize GPS and other technologies.

33

Measuring Temperature

Scientists use thermometers to measure the temperature of substances in their labs. Invented in the 1600s, the first sealed thermometers were made of glass tubes that contained a liquid, usually alcohol or mercury. The warmer the substance, the more the liquid would expand and the farther it would climb up the tube. A scale indicated on the side of the tube allows the scientist to read the temperature.

For many years, scientists tinkered with different scales for measuring temperature. Some used the freezing and boiling points of water as the basis for their scales, while others used human body temperature as one endpoint. Today two temperature scales are commonly used: the Fahrenheit and Celsius scales. The Fahrenheit scale sets the boiling point of water at 212 degrees, and the freezing point at 32 degrees. The Celsius scale uses 100 degrees and 0 degrees for the boiling and freezing points of water.

When using a glass laboratory thermometer, keep the it upright in the liquid and don't let it touch the bottom or sides of the container. The liquid also must completely surround the base of the thermometer. When reading the thermometer, make sure you are at eye level with it to get an accurate reading.

Make Your Own Thermometer

Doctors use thermometers to measure a patient's body temperature and help diagnose potential sickness or viruses. Now you can make your own.

What You'll Need

- measuring cup
- water
- rubbing alcohol
- food coloring

- drinking straw
- clear plastic water bottle
- clay
- safety goggles

What You'll Do

1. Put on safety goggles.
2. In a measuring cup, mix ¼ cup (60 milliliters) water, ¼ cup (60 milliliters) rubbing alcohol and a few drops of food coloring.
3. Pour the liquid into a clear plastic water bottle.
4. Add the drinking straw, but do not drink the alcohol mixture.
5. Use the clay to hold the straw in place.
6. Experiment with the thermometer. What happens to the liquid if you hold it in your warm hands? What happens if you place it in ice water?

Cold Calculations

In 1848, Lord Kelvin invented a third temperature scale. It set as zero the lowest possible temperature that could ever exist, called "absolute zero." It is equal to -459.69 degrees Fahrenheit or -273.16 degrees Celsius. There are no negative numbers in the Kelvin scale.

Lord Kelvin
1824 – 1907

Tools for Analyzing and Communicating

Long before computers and calculators, scientists used simple tools to analyze their data: pens, paper, and people. In the 1750s, three scientists, including Nicole-Reine Lepaute, sat at a table in Paris with goose quills, pens made of feathers, and paper. Their goal was to more accurately predict when Halley's comet would fly closest to the sun. The comet, named for astronomer Edmond Halley, reappears every 75 or 76 years. Doing the math by hand, Lepaute and her colleagues worked for five months before determining the comet would fly closest to the sun in spring 1758.

Nicole-Reine Lepau

1723 – 1788

Halley's Comet crosses the Milky Way in 1986.

Modern scientists use sophisticated tools to analyze data from their experiments including calculators and computers. Calculators perform many mathematic functions from simple addition to subtraction to calculus and trigonometry.

Tools You Can Count On

Since the beginning of time people have used tools to help them perform calculations. These could be their fingers, sticks, pebbles, or pieces of grain. The abacus is a mechanical calculator made of metal and beads, which was probably invented in the Middle East in the early Middle Ages. Merchants used the tool to help with calculations, and the tool spread along trade routes to Europe and Asia.

Computers also are used to create visual representations of data. Graphs and charts help scientists see relationships between their **variables**, the parts of an experiment that change. This helps scientists draw conclusions about whether a hypothesis was correct.

Computers also help scientists communicate their results. Using word processing programs, they write scientific papers, which are published in academic journals. Journals are scholarly magazines where scientists share their research with others.

Scientists also may use the Internet to share their data from experiments. The Internet is a system of computer networks all connected together like a spider web.

Communication Tools

Scientific publications boomed during the 16th and 17th centuries. Scientists shared their discoveries by writing letters to each other or by publishing entire books of their work, which were printed on early printing presses. By 1660 several scientists formed a group called the Royal Society of London. In 1665, the group published the first scientific journal: *The Philosophical Transactions of the Royal Society*.

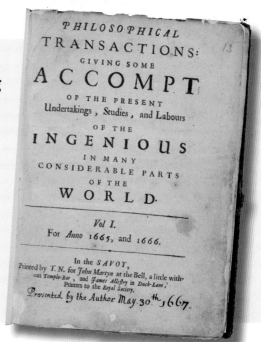

World Wide Web

The United States military created the Internet in the 1960s. In 1965, a telephone line connected two computers from opposite sides of the country. As more and more computers became connected, people thought the connections looked like a web, which may have led to the name World Wide Web. Today's scientists use the Internet to perform research and share their findings.

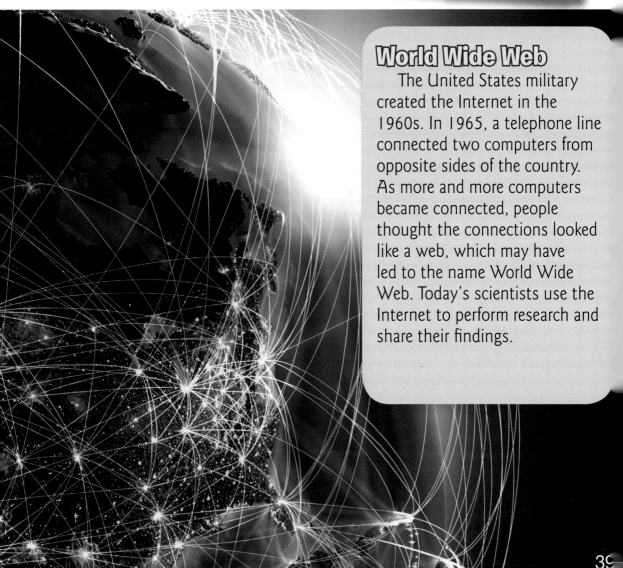

Future Tools

Technology and invention constantly change tools scientists use. Today, many scientists use the Global Positioning System (GPS), a group of satellites that circle the Earth. The United States military operates the GPS system, but today anyone can use it in cars and on cell phones to find their way.

To learn more about different animals, wildlife biologists use GPS. Take basking sharks, for example. Even though these giants are one of the biggest creatures in the sea, scientists know little about them. This is a major problem, since the number of basking sharks is declining. Scientists hope GPS tags will solve the mystery. They attach tags near sharks' dorsal fins. The tags store information

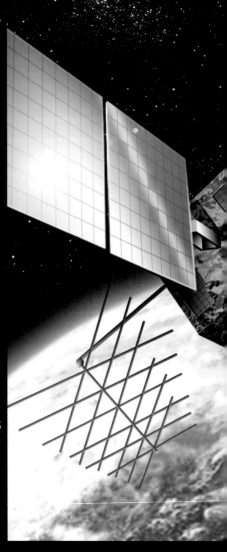

GPS systems rely on the Doppler Effect. The change in frequency of signals from the satellites helps identify locations.

about the shark's location, travels, and the depth at which they swim. When the shark surfaces, the tag transmits the information to satellites.

The tool already has led to new discoveries. Scientists used to think basking sharks made their homes in small areas, but through GPS tags, they learned that basking sharks migrate thousands of miles to spend the winter in warmer climates.

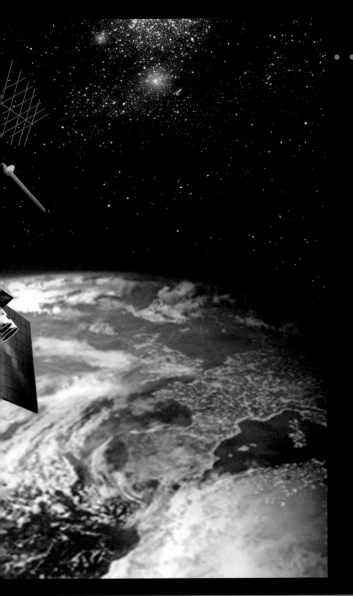

Sloth Sighting

Sloths survive by camouflaging themselves in the forest. Because they are so hard to see, scientists know little about how they behave in the wild. GPS promises to change this. Zoologist Becky Cliffe outfits sloths in Costa Rica with tiny backpacks that record what the creatures do 24 hours a day. The GPS tags in the backpacks tell Cliffe where sloths are as they go about their daily routines.

How does satellite tracking work?

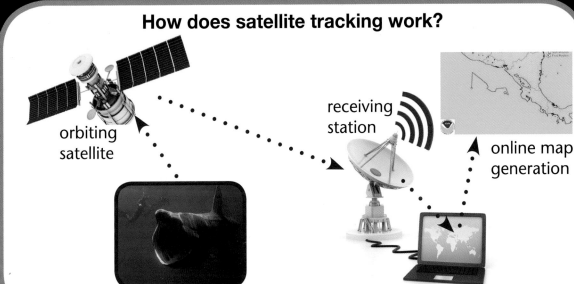

orbiting satellite

receiving station

online map generation

basking shark with GPS tag

data processing

The military first used drones, remotely piloted airplanes, to gather information and even fire weapons. Today, drones have become so inexpensive people buy them and fly them for fun. Now scientists are recognizing the benefits of this new tool.

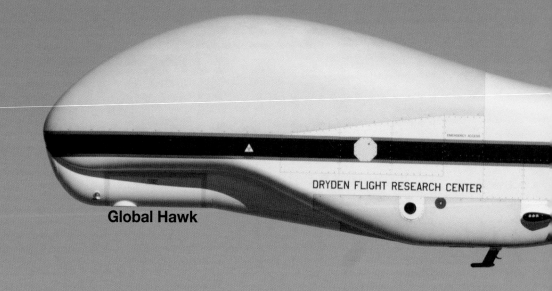

Global Hawk

DRYDEN FLIGHT RESEARCH CENTER

NASA scientists fly Global Hawks outfitted with six science instruments into storms to learn how hurricanes form in the Atlantic. The agency also has used five-pound (2.3 kilogram) drones to take samples of toxic gas from a volcano in Chile. Hurricanes and volcanoes are two situations normally too dangerous for scientists to study up close. Drones allow scientists to perform this dangerous work more safely.

Bird's Eye View

Wildlife biologists use drones too. Dr. Erick Greene has used remotely piloted helicopters with cameras to peer into osprey nests located atop high poles. The drones allow him to check on the eggs and see if they hatch.

As technology changes, so do science tools. From pens and paper to drones, science tools do the same job: helping scientists' extend their abilities. Tools help scientists see better, hear better, and perform more precise experiments. They help scientists test their hypotheses and analyze their results. Together, these tools of the trade unlock new discoveries.

Simple Tools, Sensational Discoveries

Even the simplest tools can yield big discoveries. Archaeologists and paleontologists use common items like brushes, shovels, and dustpans to find fossils and the remains of life from long ago. In South Africa, scientists used these tools to gather an amazing find: the oldest-known human ancestor, Homo naledi. Found in a limestone cave, Homo naledi may be 2.8 million years old.

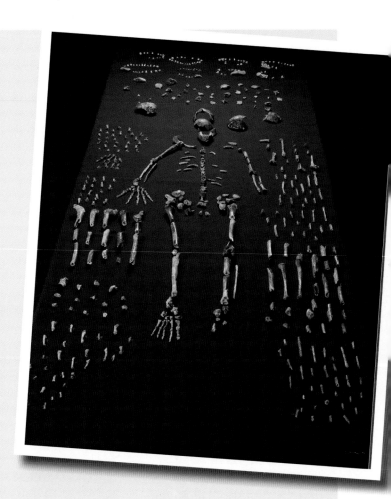

Becoming a Scientist

Scientists study many different things, and each scientific field has its own requirements. If you are interested in science, here are a few things you can do to prepare yourself.

Read books about different scientists and fields of study to learn what interests you. Do you want to be an astronaut like Sally Ride? Or would you rather study wildlife?

Watch movies and TV shows about science and scientists. Which do you most enjoy?

Take field trips to museums, zoos, natural parks, and other places that will help you explore science careers.

Sign up for science programs and activities at your school, such as the science fair or a robotics league.

On your own, practice observing the world around you, asking questions, and performing experiments.

Tinker and build your own inventions.

Find a mentor, a scientist who works in a field you might enjoy, and ask that person questions about his or her work.

Never give up!

Glossary

atoms (AT-uhms): the smallest parts of an element that has the same properties as that element; all matter is made up of atoms

data (DAY-tuh): pieces of information

electron (i-LEK-trahn): a tiny particle that circles the nucleus, or center, of an atom; it is negatively charged

genes (jeens): parts of a cell that give the directions for making a living thing; genes are passed from parents to children

hypothesis (hye-PAH-thi-sis): a testable answer to a science question

infrasonic (in-fruh-SAH-nik): too low in pitch for humans to hear

lens (lenz): a piece of curved glass or plastic that brings together or spreads light to make things appear larger or clearer

mass (mas): the amount of matter an object contains

molecule (MAH-luh-kyool): the smallest unit of a chemical that has its chemical properties; molecules are made of atoms

observation (ahb-zur-VAY-shuhn): something a scientist notices by watching carefully

slide (slide): when using a microscope, a small piece of plastic or glass used to hold a specimen

specimen (SPES-uh-muhn): a sample or example of something

theory (THEER-ee): a statement supported by facts explaining why or how something happens

variables (VAIR-ee-uh-buhlz): in science, something that changes

volume (VAHL-yoom): amount of space taken up by an object

Index

Show What You Know

1. Why do scientists use scientific tools?
2. Discuss three different ways scientists use computers in their work.
3. What are some ways to stay safe while working in a laboratory?
4. What are the two major functions of laboratory tools?
5. How have new technologies influenced science tools?

Websites to Visit

http://billnye.com/?billnyeresourcetax=home-demos

www.dartmouth.edu/~chemlab/techniques/buret.html

http://dev.nsta.org/ssc/tech.asp

About the Author

Kirsten W. Larson spent six years at NASA before writing for young people. She is the author of more than 16 books and a dozen articles about space potties, animal vampires, mammoth bones, and everything in between. She and her family live far too close to the San Andreas Fault in Southern California. Learn more at kirsten-w-larson.com.

Meet The Author!
www.meetREMauthors.com

www.rourkeeducationalmedia.com

Cover and title page: microscope and laptop/testube © Africa Studio, satellite © Johan Swanepoel, stethoscope © lenetstan, telescope © Triff, stopwatch © Rosie Apples; page 4-5 © frentusha, emerald © emerald © D.O.F; page 6 telescope © Mike Young, Uranus courtesy of NASA; page 8-9 © Huntstock. com; page 10 © jargon, page 10-11 © Neustockimages, page 11 microscope © Onur Döngel; page 12 microscope © Berents, page 13 snowflake © Kichigin, microscope © Neustockimages; page 16 top Image courtesy of NOAA Okeanos Explorer Program, inset © son, page 17 Image courtesy of NASA; page 18-19 © amrishw, page 18 inset photo © The Official CTBTO Photostream; page 20 Watson courtesy of National Institutes of Health, page 21 Crick © Marc Lieberman, page 21 template © Science Museum London _ Science and Society Picture Library; page 22 © Tinydevil, page 23 map courtesy NOAA; page 24-25 © main photo Kanate, satellite inset © qingqing; page 26 © archer fish photo © Vladimir Wrangel, illustration © Panaiotidi, page 27 © Lisa F. Young; page 28 © Michal Kowalski, page 29 © Blend Images; page 30 right © Svetlana Radayeva, left © phlox, page 31 © auremar; page 32 © Dantesattic, page 33 courtesy of United States Federal Government; page 34 © AlenD; page 36-37 courtesy of NASA, page 37 abacus © YuryZap; page 38 © NAN728, page 38-39 © Anton Balazh, page 39 top © Henry Oldenburg; page 40-41 © edobric, page 41 bottom map © Olinchuk, basking shark released into the public domain by its author, Chris Gotschalk © dangdumrong, satellite © bluebay,, page 41 top sloth © dangdumrong; page 42-43 NASA Photo / Tom Mlller, page 43 © Nancy Hochmuth; page 45 © Vector

Edited by: Keli Sipperley

Cover and Interior design by: Nicola Stratford   www.nicolastratford.com

Library of Congress PCN Data

Tools of The Trade: Using Scientific Equipment / Kirsten Larson
(Let's Explore Science)
ISBN 978-1-68191-400-8 (hard cover)
ISBN 978-1-68191-442-8 (soft cover)
ISBN 978-1-68191-481-7 (e-Book)
Library of Congress Control Number: 2015951567

Also Available as:

ROURKE'S
e-Books

Printed in the United States of America, North Mankato, Minnesota